DIFFERENTIATING NON-DISTRACTION AND SO FORTH

AN ASPECT OF TRAINING IN THOROUGH CUT

TONY DUFF

PADMA KARPO TRANSLATION COMMITTEE

This text is secret and should not be shown to those who have not had the necessary introduction and instructions of the Thorough Cut system of Dzogchen meditation. If you have not had the necessary instructions, reading this text can be harmful to your spiritual health! Seal. Seal. Seal.

First edition, November 1996
Second edition, January 2008
ISBN: 978-9937-9031-2-7

Janson typeface with diacritical marks and
Tibetan Classic typeface
Designed and created by Tony Duff
Tibetan Computer Company
http://www.tibet.dk/tcc

Produced, Printed, and Published by
Padma Karpo Translation Committee
P.O. Box 4957
Kathmandu
NEPAL

Web-site and e-mail contact through:
http://www.tibet.dk/pktc
or search Padma Karpo Translation Committee on the web.

CONTENTS

INTRODUCTION

This is a short but very clear text containing a particular type of instruction found in Great Completion teachings called "differentiations[1]". The text was taught to me by Tsoknyi Rinpoche in 1996. We have not been able to find out who the author though not knowing the author is not regarded as a problem with the text because it does contain authentic teaching of the Thorough Cut system.

Differentiations are an important part of the oral transmission of Great Completion[2] dharma. The topic is generally very secret and passed only orally from one person to another. The text here makes important points in relation to differentiations though does not go into certain topics that would make it too secret to publish. Therefore, the translation has been made available by us though it is intended only for

---

[1] Tib. shan 'byed. This term means more than to make a distinction between two things. It means to thoroughly differentiate two things, putting each one in its own, respective place.

[2] Tib. rdzogs pa chen po. Dzogchen.

people who have the instructions for the practice of the higher tantras and should not be passed around or discussed with those who have not.

There are several types of differentiations, for example the ones that differentiate between consciousness and wisdom. The ones in this text were given in relation to the practice of Thorough Cut. The text deals with three differentiations made in relation to non-distraction—which is one of the points of both essence Mahamudra and innermost Great Completion—and then with the key point of differentiating mind and wisdom[3]. They are as follows.

> 1. Non-distraction of Great Completion practice is differentiated from stupid shamatha[4]. Stupid shamatha is an indeterminate state, one which creates causes for deep stupidity.

> 2. Non-distraction of Great Completion practice is differentiated from true shamatha. True shamatha here is defined according to the Vajra Vehicle approach, not the Sutra Vehicle approach. In the sutra approach it would be about the ability to stay one-pointedly focussed. Here it is about the quality of a mind which is one-pointedly

---

[3] "Mind" throughout this book translates the Tibetan word "sems" which refers only to the complicated knower that is the mind of cyclic existence. It sits in contrast to the various words such as "wisdom" and "rigpa" that refer to its core, which has no duality and is the mind of the buddhas.

[4] Tib. zhi lkugs or zhi gnas lkug po.

focussed and that particular quality is defined. This particular shamatha comes about through investigation of the mind which gives a sense of its emptiness but which has not realized the actual emptiness of mind. This shamatha provides a feeling of peace and can be a cause of vipashyana so it can be useful to a practitioner. The non-distraction involved in it is not the same as the non-distraction of the unified shamatha-vipashyana that is the aim of Mahamudra and Great Completion practice.

3. Non-distraction of Great Completion practice is differentiated from a shamatha focussed on alaya-consciousness which, in its vastness and bareness, has an element of emptiness to it. This kind of shamatha focusses on the emptiness aspect and in doing so does not have the luminosity aspect needed with it.

4. Following these, the author points out that this brings the discussion to the point of the crucial differentiation that must be made, the differentiation between dualistic, samsaric mind—which all the states of non-distraction discussed so far have involved, even if they are increasingly subtle—and the actual mind of the buddhas, called wisdom and various other names in the meditation systems of essence Mahamudra and Thorough Cut. His short instruction that follows will not need further commentary for anyone who has already had the introduction to the nature of mind; introduction to the nature of mind is needed for these instructions to be understood.

Our Supports for Study

I have been encouraged over the years by all of my teachers and gurus to pass on some of the knowledge I have accumulated in a lifetime dedicated to the study and practice, primarily through the Tibetan Buddhist tradition, of Buddhism. On the one hand they have encouraged me to teach. On the other hand, they are concerned that, while many general books on Buddhism have been and are being published, there are few books that present the actual texts of the tradition. They and many other, closely involved people have encouraged me to make and publish high quality translations of individual texts of the tradition.

In general, we have published a wide range of books that present the important literature of Tibetan Buddhism. In particular, this book is about the most profound level of Great Completion teachings and we have published many of the important texts of that system, with each one carefully selected to inform about a particular aspect of that teaching. We prepared this book because the text in it, which is about a specific aspect of Thorough Cut teachings, acts as a support for our other texts that lay out the whole system of that teaching. We would recommend reading it in conjunction with our publications *The Feature of the Glorious, Expert King* by Patrul Rinpoche, *About the Three Lines* by Dodrupchen III, *Alchemy of Accomplishment* by Dudjom Jigdral Yeshe Dorje, *Hinting at Dzogchen* by Tony Duff, *Peak Doorways to Emancipation* by Shakya Shri, and so on. These books are all essen-

The principal lineage teachers of innermost Great Completion
as it came into Tibet including Garab Dorje, the source of the
teaching in general and the Three Lines teaching in particular.
Garab Dorje above left, Manjushrimitra above right,
Vimalamitra below left, Shri Singha below right of
Padmasambhava in the centre. Mural on the wall of Dzogchen
Monastery, Tibet, 2007. Photograph by the author.

tial reading for Thorough Cut practitioners, and we are adding other, similar titles all the time.

All in all, you will find many books both for free and for sale on our web-site, all of them prepared to the highest level of quality. Many of our books are available not only on paper but as electronic editions that can be downloaded, and all of them are prepared to the highest level of quality. We encourage you to look at our web-site to see what we have; the address is on the copyright page at the front of this book. Major book sellers also carry our paper editions.

It has also been a project of ours to make tools that non-Tibetans and Tibetans alike could use for the study and translation of Tibetan texts. As part of that project, we prepare electronic editions of Tibetan texts in the Tibetan Text input office of the Padma Karpo Translation Committee and make them available to the world. Tibetan texts are often corrupt so we make a special point of carefully correcting our work before making it available through our web-site. Thus, our electronic texts are not careless productions like most Tibetan texts found on the web but are highly reliable editions that can be used by non-scholars and scholars alike. Moreover, many of the texts are free. The Tibetan text for this book is available for download as a free, electronic edition. It is also included at the back of the book as an aid to serious study.

Our electronic texts can be read, searched, and so on, using our Tibetan software. The software can be used to set up a reference library of these texts and then used to read and even research them quickly and easily. The software, called

TibetD and TibetDoc, has many special features that make it useful not only for reading but also for understanding and even translating texts. One key feature is that you can highlight a Tibetan term in a text then look it up immediately in any of our electronic dictionaries. We suggest the highly acclaimed *Illuminator Tibetan-English Dictionary* as the best dictionary for the purpose. As with all of our publications, the software and electronic texts can be obtained from our web-site whose address is on the copyright page at the front of the book.

Health Warning

The text here is about a subject that is kept secret. Therefore, I have translated the text as it is, providing enough notes so that someone who does understand the meaning could understand the translation without mistake. However, I have deliberately not given any further explanation of or commentary to the meaning. Anyone who has had these teachings in person will be able to understand them or at least go to their teacher and ask for further explanation. Anyone who has heard these teachings in person from a qualified teacher, and especially who has had the introduction to the nature of mind[5] around which the teachings hinge, please use and enjoy the texts as you will. However, if you have not heard these teachings and if you have not had a proper introduction to the nature of your mind, you would be better off not reading this book but seeking out someone who could teach it to you.

---

[5] Introduction to the nature of mind is mostly mis-translated these days as "pointing out" instruction.

These days there are both non-Tibetans and Tibetans who can do that for you and who are available in many countries across our planet. In short, the contents of this book could be dangerous to your spiritual health if you are not ready for it, so exercise care.

These days, in the times of rampant globalization, these deep secrets have become very public. That is not necessarily a good thing. For example, I have many times in the last few years run into young men who are extremely confident of their understanding of the meaning of these profound systems but who just spout words that they have read in books. Unfortunately, they have read the books and know the words but have not contacted the inner meaning that the books are intended to be merely a pointer towards. The solidity of their minds is noticeable and not being helped by reading these things that they are not ready for and should not be reading.

My best wishes to all of you.
May you preserve the state!

Lama Tony Duff
Padma Karpo Translation Committee
Swayambunath,
Nepal
January, 2008

DIFFERENTIATING NON-DISTRACTION AND SO FORTH

Non-distraction of itself is definitely not the actuality of the authentic[6]. There are four approaches to non-distraction when the practitioner merges the practice of non-distraction with day and night around the clock practice, as follows.

1. That which is not shamatha in the slightest, referred to either as "indeterminate equanimity"[7] or "stupid shamatha", is dwelling in a state of not knowing what is happening or what you are doing. Afterwards, when you have returned to a state where you are once again apprehending with mindfulness, you will not know what the content of that earlier state

---

[6] The authentic is a name used in both sutras and tantras for what is the real situation. It is what is realized by buddhas. It's actuality is how it actually sits.

[7] Equanimity means an even state of mind, one which is not agitated. You can get it for example by sitting in a hot bath for some time. Indeterminate means that it is has not specific quality to it. It is neither virtuous or not virtuous. It leads nowhere, in other words.

was nor for how long you stayed within it; while you were in it, you had cut yourself off from everything in a state of stupefaction. If you were to work at familiarizing yourself with this kind of shamatha, you would attempt to develop it further and further until you were mixed with it day and night. The more that you habituated yourself to it, the more that your mindstream would turn cloudy and have a quality of being dumbfounded in the present life and, if unless you had the good friends of virtue and discipline accompanying it, it would cause you to take birth as an animal-type migrator in future times, albeit one whose mind has the factor of abiding present.

2. When, in the state of shamatha, you search the dwelling mind, that is, you examine it to try to find the three things arising, abiding, and going, and so on, and do not find them at all, then your mind becomes empty in the sense of being freed of three-fold birth, cessation, and abiding. However, the issue of "being empty" has not been properly determined therefore the shamatha is referred to as "possessing mere mindfulness, mere awareness[8], and mere luminosity". What is that like? It is said to be an appearance of bliss which does have the factor of experiencing, and that factor of experiencing is a luminous awareness that cannot be described. This is

---

[8] It has become popular to translate "rigpa" with awareness but that is a very bad translation that shows no understanding of what rigpa actually is. In this book "awareness" is always used to translate Tib. shes which is the general term for the mere registering capacity of mind, that is, "awareness", whether as dualistic consciousness or non-dualistic wisdom. Here the author is using it to mean the consciousness in general of samsaric mind.

actual shamatha and, when you work at familiarizing yourself with it, that also will progress onto your being mixed it with day and night.

That shamatha, moreover, is not the wisdom of vipashyana, not the essence of mind, and not realization. It is the root of every one of the worldly types of concentration and it is also referred to as "shamatha, the cause of vipashyana". Nevertheless, because Great Completion is a system in which the meditation is encountered on top of the view, rigpa's "natural absorption" style of meditation has no need of shamatha's mere calmness, and therefore shamatha is a completely unnecessary requisite.

3. In the case of alaya consciousness being what will be mixed with day and night, there is this. You have dissolved the previous type of shamatha's factor of experiencing that is a luminous awareness and expanded out into an enormous, empty kind of field. That field lacks the cause of self-fixation. Familiarization with that state will progress on to your being mixed with it around the clock. In this, the mere temporary experience of a factor of emptiness which is vast but only empty is the experience of being situated in a blankness which has none of self-arising rigpa's factor of luminosity whatsoever.

For all three of the cases mentioned so far, no matter what else they might be, it is necessary to make the differentiation that they are, of mind and rigpa, not rigpa but mind with a factor of abiding.

4. The fourth one is familiarization that leads to luminosity being mixed with around the clock. When the factor of clinging that is involved in that previous, enormous field of bare emptiness is purified out, the self-arising wisdom essence that shines like the sun comes forth. This is emptiness free of every elaboration which is not a one-sided emptiness[9], which is non-dual with the wisdom of rigpa. It is called "wisdom" because it knows everything there is and is called "rigpa" because it has direct knowledge of everything there is. It has the quality of a the most primordial type of knowing so is called "primordial awareness"[10]. This wisdom knower which, unlike the dualistic mind type of knower, is without the slightest dependence on an object and without the slightest amount of grasped-grasping[11] and clinging to true existence, is present as a self-illumination that is similar to spilled mercury that has spread everywhere in minute droplets[12].

---

[9] A one-sided emptiness is one in which the emptiness factor has become predominant. The authentic is not weighted in favour of emptiness.

[10] This has to be understood like this. It has the quality of the most primordial knowing. Therefore, the Buddha called it jñāna, knowing and that was translated into Tibetan with "primordial knowing" or "primordial awareness". In English, it is usually translated as "wisdom" though the meaning just given has to be understood for it.

[11] See glossary.

[12] The image is that the mercury goes everywhere but each droplet remains distinct. It is all-pervasive but there is no blurring of one piece into another. Wisdom's knowing is all perva-
(continued...)

You can call it "self-arising rigpa" but it means the same thing.

To do the practice of that key point, neither the mind possessing the factor of experience that is mere luminosity, mere awareness helps, nor the space-like, enormous emptiness which does not have the factor of rigpa at all, helps. Therefore, we meet the key point of needing to differentiate mind and rigpa!

The nature of mind[13] is that it mingles with its object in the same way that water and its atoms are co-mingled. Clinging and attaching to its object as it does, it grasps its way into deep solidification[14]. If there is no object, mind cannot give birth to discursive thoughts. It is something that has moment to moment creation in a process of arising and cessation.

The wisdom which is rigpa is not dependent on an object; object-less it self-illuminates. It knows objects but merely knows them and does not grasp at them. Not clinging and not entering deep solidification, it has an illusory, dream-like

---

[12](...continued)
sive, knowing every item simultaneously yet distinctly, without any mix-up.

[13] Again, this is referring to samsaric mind and not to more enlightened types of knower.

[14] Tib. aa 'thas. Deep solidification is how most samsaric minds operate. They do not merely live in dualistic ways of knowing but they heavily solidify all of what they know into the perception of a solidly real existence.

style of knowing. Things are known as the mere play or self-liveliness of the wisdom thus, after the instant in which they are known, they pass into purification in self-liberation over the rigpa, like a drawing on water. Therefore, the widsom does lose itself in these mere objects-to-be-known but experiences itself. That gives you the basis for how wisdom should be differentiated from mind.

This was heard from the mouth of the kind guru.

Translated after receiving instruction on the text from Tsoknyi Rinpoche, by Tony Duff of the Padma Karpo Translation Committee, September 4, 1996, at Swayambunath, Kathmandu, Nepal.

GLOSSARY

Actuality, Tib. gnas lugs: how things are, the way things are, how things sit in any given situation as opposed to how they might appear.

Alaya, Tib. kun gzhi: this term, if translated, is usually translated as all-base or thereabouts. It means a range that underlies something else; an underlying basis for something else. It is used in several different ways in the Buddhist teaching and changes to a different meaning in case. All in all, it means a space of mind that underlies many other minds that come from it.

Clarity, Skt. vara, Tib. gsal ba: when you see this term, it should be understood as an abbreviation of the full term in Tibetan, 'od gsal ba, which is usually translated as luminosity. It is not another factor of mind distinct from luminosity but merely a convenient abbreviation in both Indian and Tibetan dharma language for the longer term, luminosity. See "Luminosity" in this glossary for more.

Clinging, Tib. zhen pa: dualistic mind that takes things that are not true, not pure, as being true, pure, etcetera and then, because of seeing them as highly desirable attaches itself or clings to those things. It acts a kind of glue that keeps you with the things of cyclic existence, such as thoughts.

Cyclic existence, Tib. 'khor ba: saṃsāra: the type of existence that sentient beings have which is that continue on from one existence to another, always within the enclosure of births that are produced by ignorance and experienced as unsatisfactory.

Discursive thought, Tib. rnam rtog: this means more than just the superficial thought that is heard as a voice in the head. It includes the entirety of conceptual process that arises due to mind contacting any object of any of the senses. Discursive thought here translates from the Sanskrit original where the meaning is "conceptual thought that arises from the mind wandering among the various superficies perceived in the doors of the senses".

Essence, Tib. ngo bo: a key term used throughout Buddhist theory. The original in Sanskrit and the term in Tibetan, too, has both meanings of "essence" and "entity". In some situations the term has more the first meaning and in others, the second. For example, when speaking of mind and mind's essence, it is referring to the core or essential part within mind. On the other hand, when speaking of fire or some other thing, there is the entity, fire, and so on, and its characteristics, such as heat, and so on; in this case, it is not an essence but an entity.

Grasped-grasping, Tib. gzung 'dzin: When mind is turned outwardly as it is in the normal operation of dualistic mind, it has developed two faces that appear simultaneously. Special names are given to these two faces: mind appearing in the form of the external object being referenced is called "that which is grasped". Mind appearing in the form of the consciousness that is referencing it is called "the grasper" or "grasping" of it. Thus, there is the pair of terms "grasped-grasper" or "grasped-grasping". When these two terms are used, it alerts you immediately to the fact that a Mind Only style of presentation is being discussed and it should bring the whole flavour of Mind Only along with it. This pair of terms pervades Mind Only, Madhyamaka, and tantric writings and is exceptionally important in all of them.

The solidified duality of grasped and grasper is nothing but an invention of dualistic thought. It has that kind of character or characteristic.

Note that you could substitute the word "apprehended" for "grasped" and "apprehender" for "grasper" or "grasping" and that would reflect one connotation of the original Indian terminology.

Liveliness, Tib. rtsal: another key term in Mahāmudrā and Great Completion. The term means the potential that something contains for it to produce or display some kind of expression. For example, a baby horse has the innate ability that will later come out as its liveliness of galloping and prancing as a steed. However, the term also is used in situations where the energy is actually happening, that is, it is not mere potential any more but is the energy at the time of its expression. The term that seems to fit correctly in English is "spunk", unfortunately not many people know this word well. It is the potential and the expression of dynamic display that something has within it.

Luminosity, Skt. prabhāsvara, Tib. 'od gsal ba: the core of mind, called mind's essence, has two aspects, parts, or factors as they are called. One is emptiness and the other is knowing. Luminosity is a metaphor for the fundamental knowing quality of the essence of mind. It is sometimes translated as "clear light" but that is a mistake that comes from not understanding how the words of the Tibetan go together. It does not refer to a light that is clear but refers to the illuminative property which is the hallmark of mind. Mind knows, that is what it does. Thus, it has the property of luminosity which knows its own content. Both in Sanskrit and Tibetan Buddhist literature, the term is frequently abbreviated just to gsal ba, "clarity", with the same meaning.

Mind, Tib. sems: conventional minding which occurs because there is ignorance.

Mindfulness, Tib. dran pa: the ability to keep mind on an object of the senses. With alertness, it is one of the two causes of developing śhamatha.

Rigpa, Tib. rig pa: The singularly most important term in the whole of Great Completion and Mahāmudrā. This is the term used to indicate enlightened mind as experienced by the practitioner on the path of these practices. The term itself specifically refers to the dynamic knowing quality of mind. It absolutely does not mean a simple registering, as implied by the word "awareness" which unfortunately is often used to translate this term. There is no word in English that exactly matches it, unfortunately, though the idea of "seeing" or "insight on the spot" is very close. Proof of this is found in the fact that the original Sanskrit term "vidyā" is actually the root of all words in English that start with "vid" and mean "to see", for example, "video". Chogyam Trungpa Rinpoche, who was particular skilled at getting Tibetan words into English, also stated that this term rigpa really did not have a good equivalent in English, though "insight" he thought was the closest. My own conclusion after hearing extensive teachings on these subjects is that rigpa is just best left untranslated. However, it will be helpful in reading the text to understanding the meaning as just given. Note that rigpa has both noun and verb forms.

Shamatha, Tib. gzhi gnas: one of the two main practices of meditation required in the Buddhist system for gaining insight into reality. It develops one-pointedness of mind. The completion of the practice is a mind that sits stably on its object without any effort. Essentially, it allows the other practice, vipaśhyanā, to focus on its object unwaveringly.

Thorough Cut, Tib. khregs chod: the Dzogchen system has several levels to it. The innermost level has two levels, the first is called Thregcho which literally translates as Thorough Cut and the second is called Thogal which literally translates as Leaping Over at the Top. The meaning of Thregcho has been misunderstood and hence mistranslated. The meaning is clearly explained in the *Illuminator Tibetan-English Dictionary*; it gives the following.

> "The Thorough Cut is a system in which the solidification that sentient beings produce by having rational minds which grasp at a perceived object and perceiving subject is sliced through so as to get the underlying reality which has always been present in the essence of mind and which is called Alpha Purity in this system of teachings. For this reason Thorough Cut is also known as Alpha Purity Thorough Cut."

The etymology of the word is explained in the Great Completion System either as ཁྲེགས་སུ་ཆོད་པ་ or ཁྲེགས་གོ་ཆོད་པ་. In either case, the term ཆོད་པ་ is the standard intransitive verb meaning "for something to be cut through". As the intransitive root, it simply comes to mean "a cut", a type of cut. Some Westerners have tried to make a big deal out of the intransitive sense, suggesting that it means a past tense sense, that is, a cut which has happened. That shows a misunderstanding of Tibetan grammar. The intransitive sense here just makes it "a cut" like in English there could be all sorts of different "cuts". So this is one type of "cut". Then, in the case of ཁྲེགས་ སུ་ཆོད་པ་, ཁྲེགས་སུ་ becomes an adverb modifying the verb "to cut" and has the meaning of making the cut fully, completely.

It is explained with the example of slicing off a finger. A finger could be sliced with a sharp knife such that the cut was not quite complete and the cut off portion was left hanging. Alternatively, it could be sliced through in one, decisive movement such that the finger was completely and definitely severed. In the case of ཁྲེགས་གི་ཆོད་པ, the term ཁྲེགས་གི functions as an adverb though it is one of the many experiential terms of the Tibetan language. It has the meaning and feeling with it, of something that is doubtless, of something that is unquestionably so. A translation based on the first explanation would be "Complete Cut", "Thorough Cut", "Cutting Through", "Through Cut", "Solid Cut". A translation based on the second explanation would be "Definite Cut", "Decisive Cut".

Other translations that have been put forward for this term are: "Cutting Resistance" and "Cutting Solidity". Of these, "Cutting Resistance" is usually a translation made on the basis of students expressing the "resistance to practice", etcetera. That is a complete misunderstanding of the term: firstly the words of the term mean "Decisive Cut" or "Thorough Cut", and secondly, the term refers specifically to decisively cutting the solidification that has happened because of བློ rational mind dualizing the world into a perceived object and perceiving subject, with the result of arriving fully and directly into the alpha purity of the ground.

The Thorough Cut" gives the sense that the practitioner of this system cuts decisively through the conceptual solidification which is none other than rational mind so as to arrive directly at the essence of mind.

Vipashyana, Tib. lhag mthong: one of the two main practices of meditation required in the Buddhist system for gaining insight into reality. It is the insight that directly sees reality. It is aided by śhamatha which keeps it focussed on the reality.

Wisdom, Tib. ye shes: this terms translates the original Sanskrit, jñāna. Jñāna has many meanings but overall has the sense of just knowing. In the Buddhist usage it is very literal, meaning the most basic sense we have of knowing which is the knowing that is there from the beginning in the core of mind. Because of this meaning, the Tibetans translated it as "the particular awareness which has been there from the beginning". This has been translated into English in various ways but, as long as the meaning just mentioned is understood, that will be enough.

In the tantras, there are many methods for bringing the students to this primordial awareness. Some of them bring the student first to something which is similar to the wisdom so there is the term, simile wisdom[15]; this is often translated as example wisdom but that is being literal to the extent of losing the meaning. The simile wisdom is a similitude of the real wisdom, the actual wisdom which is shown in various ways, including by the fourth empowerment. al wisdom[16] is the opposite of simile wisdom; it is wisdom in fact, not the one which is just a similitude of the real wisdom.

---

[15] Tib. dpe'i ye shes

[16] Tib. don gyi ye shes

TIBETAN TEXT

༄༅། །མ་ཡེངས་པ་སོགས་ཀྱི་ཤན་འབྱེད་ནི། མ་ཡེངས་པ་ཆམ་ཁོ་ན་ཡང་
དག་པའི་གནས་ལུགས་གཏན་ནས་མིན་ཏེ། ཉེན་མཚན་ཁོར་ཡུག་འདྲེས་པ་
ལ་རྣམ་པ་བཞི་ཡོད་དེ། དང་པོ་ནི། ཞི་གནས་ཆམ་ཡང་མ་ཡིན་པའི་བཏང་
སྙོམས་ལུང་མ་བསྟན་ཡང་ཟེར། ཞི་གནས་ཞི་ལྷུགས་ཡང་ཟེར། དོན་ཅི་
སོང་གང་སོང་མ་གོ་བའི་དང་དུ་གནས། རྗེས་ནས་དྲན་པས་ཉེན་དུས་ཅི་རེད་
དང་ཡུན་རིང་བྱུང་ཅེ་སོང་མ་གོ་བར་ཏུན་ཞེར་ལུས་པ་དེ་ཡིན་པས་དེ་ལ་གོམས་
སོང་ན་ཉེན་མཚན་འདྲེས་འགྲོ། དེ་ལ་ཅི་ཆམ་གོམས་ཡང་རང་རྒྱུད་རྗེ་རྟོངས་
རྗེ་བླུན་དུ་འགྲོ། ཆུལ་ཁྲིམས་དང་དགེ་བའི་གྲོགས་བཟང་མེད་ན་ཕྱི་མ་དུད་
འགྲོ་སེམས་ལ་གནས་ཆ་ཡོད་པའི་རིགས་སུ་སྐྱེ་འགྲོ་བ་དེ་ཡིན་ནོ། །གཉིས་
པ་ཞི་གནས་ནི་སེམས་ཀྱི་མཚང་བཙལ་ཏེ་བྱུང་གནས་འགྲོ་གསུམ་སོ་གས
བཏགས་ནས། གང་ཡང་མ་རྟེད་པའི་སྐྱེ་འགགགས་གནས་གསུམ་དང་ཕྲལ་བའི་
སྟོང་པ་ཡང་ཡིན། སྟོང་ཐག་ཡང་མ་ཆོད་པས་དྲན་ཆམ་རིག་ཆམ་གསལ་
ཆམ་འདུག་ཟེར། ༼༧༽ དོན་ཅི་ལྟ་བུ་ཞིག་རེད་རྗེས་ན། ཟེར་མི་ཤེས་པའི་
གསལ་རིག་གི་སྟོང་ཆ་ཙན་བདེ་མོ་ཞིག་སྟུང་ཟེར་བ་དེ་ཡིན། དེ་ཞི་གནས་ཀྱི

15

རོ་བོ་མཚན་ཉིད་པ་དེ་ལ་གོམས་གྱུང་ཉིན་མཚན་འཛེས་འགྲོ། དེ་ཡང་ལྷག་
མཐོང་གི་ཡེ་ཤེས་མིན། སེམས་ཀྱི་རོ་བོ་མིན། རྟོགས་པ་མིན། འཇིག་
རྟེན་པའི་བསམ་གཏན་ཐམས་ཅད་ཀྱི་རྩ་བ་དེ་ཡིན། ལྷག་མཐོང་གི་རྒྱུ་ཞེ་
གནས་ཟེར་བ་དེ་ཡིན་ཀྱང་རྟོགས་པ་ཆེན་པོ་ལྟ་ཐོག་ནས་བསྒོམ་པ་འཚོལ་བའི་
ལུགས་ཡིན་པས་རིག་པ་རང་བབས་ཀྱི་བསམ་གཏན་སྒོམ་པ་ལས་ཞེ་གནས་ཞེ་
རྒྱུང་གི་དགོས་པ་མེད་པས་འདི་མཐོ་གལ་ཆེ་བ་ཙེ་ཡང་མེད་དོ། །གསུམ་པ་
ཀུན་གཞིའི་རྣམ་ཤེས་སྟེང་དུ་ཉིན་མཚན་འཛེས་ལུགས་ལ། སྱར་གྱི་ཞི་གནས་
དེའི་གསལ་རིག་གི་མྱོང་ཆ་དེ་ཡལ་ནས་བདག་བཟུང་བྱེད་རྒྱུ་མེད་པའི་སྟོང་པ་
ཡུག་འབྱམས་ལ་བྱུང་སོང་བའི་ངང་དུ་གོམས་སོང་ན་ཕྱིར་ཡུག་འཛེས་འགྲོ།
འདི་ལ་སྟོང་ཆ་རྒྱུང་པ་རྒྱ་ཆེན་པོའི་ཉམས་ཚམ་ལས། ⌈ ༣ ⌉ རང་བྱུང་རིག་
པའི་གསལ་ཆ་ཙེ་ཡང་མེད་པ་ཧྲད་པོར་འདུག་པ་དེ་ཡིན། དེ་གསུམ་གང་ཡིན་
ཀྱང་སེམས་དང་རིག་པ་གཉིས་ལས་སེམས་ཀྱི་གནས་ཆ་ཚམ་ལས་རིག་པ་མིན་
པ་ཤན་འབྱེད་དགོས་སོ། །བཞི་པ་འོད་གསལ་ཕྱར་ཡུག་འཛེས་པ་ནི།
སྱར་གྱི་སྟོང་རྒྱུང་ཡུག་འབྱམས་དེའི་ཞེན་ཆ་དེ་དག་ནས། ཉི་མ་ཤར་བ་ལྟ་
བུའི་རང་བྱུང་གི་ཡེ་ཤེས་རོ་བོ་སྙོམས་པ་ཐམས་ཅད་བྲལ་བའི་སྟོང་པ་དེ་སྟོང་པ་
ཕྱོགས་གཅིག་མ་ཡིན་པ། རིག་པའི་ཡེ་ཤེས་དང་གཉིས་སུ་མེད་པ། ཙེ་
ཡང་ཤེས་པ་ཡིན་པས་ཡེ་ཤེས་དང་། ཙེ་ཡང་རིག་པས་རིག་པ་ཟེར། ཡེ་
ཤེས་ཟེར་བའི་དོན་ཡེ་ནས་ཤེས་པའི་རང་བཞིན་ཅན། སེམས་ཀྱི་ཤེས་པ་ལྟ་
བུའི་ཡུལ་ལ་ལྟོས་པ་དང་། གཟུང་འཛིན་དང་བདེན་ཞེན་ཕྲ་རགས་གང་ཡང་
མེད་པ་དངུལ་རྒྱ་དྭལ་ནང་དུ་ལྦུང་བ་ལྟ་བུ་རང་གསལ་དུ་འདུག་པ་དེ་ཡིན།
རང་བྱུང་གི་རིག་པ་ཟེར་ཡང་དེ་དང་དོན་གཅིག་ཡིན། དེ་ཡིན་པའི་གནད་ཀྱི་
ཉམས་ལེན་བྱེད་རྒྱུ་སེམས་རོ་དེ་གསལ་ཚམ་རིག་ཚམ་གྱིས་མྱོང་ ⌈ ༣ ⌉ ཆ་ཚན་

དེས་ཀྱང་མི་ཕན། སྟོང་པ་ནས་མཁན་ལྟ་བུ་རིག་པའི་ཆ་ཙི་ཡང་མེད་པའི་
སྟོང་འབུམས་དེས་ཀྱང་མི་ཕན་པས་སེམས་རིག་ཤན་འབྱེད་དགོས་པའི་གནད་དེ་
ལ་ཐུག །སེམས་ཀྱི་རང་བཞིན་དེ་ནི་རྒྱུ་རྐྱལ་དང་འབྲེས་པ་ལྟར་ཡུལ་དང་
འབྲེས། དེ་ལ་ཞེན་ཅིང་ཆགས་ལ་འཐབས་སུ་འཛིན་པ་དེ་ཡིན། ཡུལ་མེད་
ན་སེམས་ཀྱིས་རྣམ་རྟོག་སྐྱེ་མི་ཤེས། སྐད་ཅིག་སྐད་ཅིག་གི་སྐྱེ་འགག་བྱེད་པ
ཅན་ཡིན། རིག་པའི་ཡེ་ཤེས་ནི། ཡུལ་ལ་མི་ལྟོས་པ། ཡུལ་མེད་རང་
གསལ་ཡིན། ཡུལ་ཤེས་ཀྱང་དེ་ལ་ཤེས་ཚམ་ལས་ཡུལ་དེ་ལ་མི་འཛིན།
མི་ཞེན་ཨ་མི་འཐབས་པར་སྐྱུ་མ་རྐྲི་ལམ་ལྟ་བུར་ཤེས་སོ། །ཡེ་ཤེས་ཀྱི་རང་
རྒྱལ་ལམ་རོལ་པ་ཚམ་དུ་ཤེས་པས། ཤེས་པའི་དུས་སྐད་ཅིག་དེ་ནས་རིག་
ཐོག་ཏུ་རྒྱལ་རེ་མི་བྲིས་པ་ལྟར་རང་གྲོལ་དུ་དག་འགྲོ་བ་ཡིན་པས་འདི་དག་གོ
ཡུལ་ཚམ་དུ་མ་ཤོར་བར་རང་གི་སྙིང་ཐོག་ནས་ཤན་འབྱེད་དགོས་ཤེས་རྗེན་ཅན
བླ་མའི་ཞལ་ནས་ཐོས་སོ།། ||

INDEX

19